Be a Leader in All that You Do

Work/Balance/Life

A Self-Exam of your
Leadership Effectiveness

Written By:

Charisse J. Rudolph
Winner of the Leadership Award for Contribution to Women.

https://equineheartconnection.com

Editorial supervision: Billie Jo Youmans, billiejoyoumans@gmail.com
Front cover design: Humble Nation

Library of Congress Cataloging- in- Publication Data

Rudolph, Charisse,
Be a Leader in All that You Do, A Self-Exam of your Leadership Effectiveness
Charisse Rudolph

ISBN – 13:979-1517091750 ISBN – 10:1517091756
Leadership, Women, Communication, Leadership Assessment.

The Leaders Code of Ethics

~~~~~~

- I will say what I mean and mean what I say.

- If someone makes a mistake, I will only speak about the action not about their personal self-worth.

- I will always be consistent with my requests.

- I will speak without sarcasm or ridicule.

- I will not patronize or be condescending.

- I will lead by example.

- I will not play favorites, hold a grudge, argue or justify.

- Whining is never allowed.

- I will be patient, yet firm.

- I will be respectful to others.

- If I have an upset, I will allow myself time to find balance before I deal with the next thing on my agenda.

- I will delegate instead of procrastinate.

- I will say yes with passion, or no without regret.

- I will stay true to the **"Leadership Code of Ethics"** striving everyday to improve my leadership skills. I will give the most efficient service I am capable of giving, staying true to who I am, to those who seek my leadership. I will walk in balance, remembering to lead my life, so life will not lead me.

NAME _____   DATE _____

DEDICATION

- This book is dedicated to all those who wear more than one hat; breadwinner, homemaker, spouse and parent.

- To the single parents raising families.

- To my mom, who came from the era of "I LOVE LUCY," never attended college, married young, raised four children and after twenty-one years of marriage, divorced and tried to cook herself into a career.

- To those like me, who struggle to stay true to themselves and lead a life with passion, instead of being led by the circumstances of life.

CONTENTS

About Charisse Rudolph,
Charisse Rudolph is fiercely committed to empowering women by sharing sound advice for positive change. Her motto is: "Lead your Life, or Life will Lead you!" Charisse was honored to receive; "The Leadership Award for Contribution to Women."

INTRODUCTION
A great leader leads by example, and through his or her example teaches others to be an effective lead

"A thought put into the mind is the beginning of a line of conduct: The thought first sends down its roots into the mind and then pushes forth into the light in the form of actions or conduct which evolve into character and destiny." James Allen

About - CHARISSE J. RUDOLPH

Charisse Rudolph is the author of "***The Art of Facilitation, with 28 Equine Assisted Activities,***" and "***Be a Leader in All that You Do, a Self-Exam of Your Leadership Effectiveness.***" She began her journey in Equine Assisted Services in 2001, wanting to bring her horses into the work with the company she co-owned, "Outdoor Learning Adventures" (OLA). OLA worked with many schools and corporations such as Disney, 20th Century Fox, General Telephone Company, Wells Fargo, etc.

Charisse joined EAGALA and took their training in 2001 and a year later, after she had founded her first non-profit for women and teens she won "The Leadership Award for Contribution to Women." Charisse began learning The Art of Facilitation in 1992 from the Wilderness Institute and Outward Bound.

In 2011, Charisse received her level two certification with EAGALA. Soon afterwards she founded "Healing Horses & Armed Forces." Learning everything she could to assist the sons and daughters that were returning from the Iraq and Afghanistan war, Charisse attended and spoke at many veteran organizations, she also worked with several military bases.

In 2013, she was certified as an Equine Specialist in Mental Health with Path Intl., and in 2014, Rising Moon Ranch became a Premier Accredited Center with Path Intl. From there she became a contractor for the Wounded Warriors Project. Soon afterwards, Charisse received her license as a mentor, coach and trainer from the HeartMath Institute and was trained in therapeutic art with, A Window between Worlds."

Charisse partners with her horses, and combines the Heartmath techniques in addition to, offering therapeutic art and drumming circles. She is an artist, painting the human-equine connection, and author of several books.

Starting in 2020, Charisse began her new adventure "**Equine Heart Connection**." **Equine Heart Connection** includes, Equine Assisted Trainings for people to sharpen up on their facilitation skills involving horses and people, equine paintings depicting the human-equine connection, and books.

INTRODUCTION

Originally, I wrote this book for women. Then I began to think about the men in my life and realized they go through similar challenges. The male and female role gets confusing for them too. Because of my realization, two minutes before I sent this book off to be published, I went through it one more time to include the men in our lives.

I have led and facilitated many leadership programs throughout the years and one of the struggles that are discussed regularly is balancing home and work. In essence, "How does a woman or a man go from being an effective leader at work, come home and have to consider his or her spouses needs and decisions?

> "It is 7:00 pm. I have worked all day and I am beat. My husband has had a full day at work as well. We both fed and put the horses away this evening, and I am feeling guilty for not having dinner ready. My mind tells me it is not necessarily the woman's job to cook, but when I don't cook my husband eats junk food, and I feel guilty."

Women and men have both come a long way. Women do everything that was once a man's obligation, and men do the work that was once seen as "women's work." Our roles get confusing with our partners in our personal lives. I see couples pop in and out of the traditional roles all the time. Most girl talk includes what our husbands did or didn't do. Each of us lives with expectations, and those are what cause most arguments.

While more men are doing domestic chores, more women are working outside the home than ever before. Coping with this change is one of the greatest challenges of our time. Women who once were dependent on men financiallyhave taken control of their own economic fates; a change that affects aspects of our social and intimate lives.

In most cases, our children are being raised with two parents working, and while economically it is helping the family, there are negative effects as well. I wrote this book so women and men can take a look at their leadership style and identify needed changes, so they don't feel overwhelmed.

Part of being a good leader is first leading your own life. If you can't lead yourself, you can't lead others. That is why I say, "Lead your life, or life will lead you." This book will take you on a journey of self-discovery. Give yourself the time to answer the questions and reflect. This will allow you to see your leadership style and make the shift you need to bring peace and harmony into your life.

QUALITIES OF AN EFFECTIVE LEADER

- An effective leader is confident.

- An effective leader leads by example.

- An effective leader has the respect of his or her team members. Team members give their all, not out of fear, but out of respect because they know they are part of something greater than their individual selves.

- An effective leader shows respect for each member of the team and values the natural gift or ability that each team member can offer.

- An effective team member realizes that each team member is part that makes a whole.

- An effective leader is only as good as his or her team. The team will only be as good as his or her ability to empower each individual to be a good leader.

- An effective leader knows how to delegate but still over sees.

- An effective leader never stops growing, always expanding their mind and knowledge.

- An effective leader has a strong positive mental attitude.

- An effective leader knows how to set goals and keep the journey alive with enthusiasm and encouragement.

- An effective leader understands boundaries, his or her own, as well as the personal boundaries of the team members.

- An effective leader knows how to address wrong actions without disrespecting the person within.

- An effective leader takes responsibility for his or her mistakes.

- An effective leader has good discipline.

- An effective leader can be anyone.

- An effective leader applies the same rules to his or her life, at work and at home.

FORWARD

Lead your life, or life will lead you. I say this quote regularly; it has been my mantra for years. What does it mean? If you don't have direction, if you don't make decisions, life will use you like a pawn. In Chess the pawn is the weakest piece in the game. You have to think of life as a game and everyone in the world is a player whether they choose to play or not. In addition, every second, life is moving forward like a stream or a river. You can't stop the flow, and if you are not moving forward, you are falling back. Choose your path, or you will get swept away by the current.

Think about your life. What do you want to do? The answer will plant the seeds for the future. If your thoughts are about what you don't have instead of what you do have, those will be the seeds that you plant. They are the seeds of not enough.

> *A thought put into the mind is the beginning of a line of conduct: The thought first sends down its roots into the mind and then pushes forth into the light in the form of, actions or conduct which evolve into character and destiny.*
> -James Allen-

Think about what the above paragraph is really saying. If you think you can ignore something that needs to be dealt with, or you are concentrating on what is wrong in your life, your thoughts are planting the wrong seeds for the future. "We reap what we sow."

Each thought is sending down roots, into the mind like a giant oak tree sends its roots into the earth. From those roots the giant oak begins a life of its own by sending up a sprout into the sunlight to grow. A thought grows into the form of actions and how you conduct your life. The very thoughts in your mind evolve into your character and become your destiny. Each thought is leading you to your future.

Part of being a good leader is first leading your own life. If you can't lead yourself, you can't be a good leader or facilitator for others.

That is why I say, "Lead your Life or Life will lead You."

ONE

How do you assume a leadership role?

I am sure you have heard the old saying, "So and so, makes a natural born leader." I say, "Rubbish," a natural born leader is someone who has been nurtured and held in high esteem for his or her efforts by a parent, teacher, or mentor. Everyone has ideas, but if you are not confident in yourself, you cannot lead. Others will not believe in you unless you believe in yourself. Here is a perfect example:

Since I co-owned a team building company for ten years, I was able to facilitate hundreds of groups. What always amazed me was how certain people were given the role of leadership. Many times, it was unspoken, and because of the team dynamics a pecking order was established unconsciously.

One group really sticks in my mind. We were working with a group of students and there was one young man in my group whom everyone listened to and followed. What was so amazing is that he always had the *worst* ideas on how to accomplish a task. Like lemmings jumping off a cliff, everyone followed his direction. There were people in the group who had much better ideas than his, but they never were heard. (By the way, being heard is *your* responsibility!)

So, why did this happen? He was confident; he spoke in a manner like he really knew what he was doing; and he always convinced everyone that he had the right answer. It didn't matter how many times his ideas didn't work.

He believed in himself so much that everyone else did as well.
He was enthusiastic, and he made a plan. He knew how to keep everyone's energy up and moving forward. He also knew the art of communicating and influencing others.

As the facilitator, I had to manipulate many of the team initiatives so everyone could see the benefit of working as a team without squishing his ego or ambition. There was a girl in the group who had little self-esteem and great ideas. The combination of the two was awesome. I had to encourage her to speak up and be heard while encouraging the young man to listen to different ideas. This group needed to learn they were a team.

So, how do you assume a leadership role? You believe in yourself, you have a positive attitude, and you don't give up. A good leader is ambitious, enthusiastic, and focused. He or she comes up with ideas to accomplish the goal. A good leader has confidence. How do you gain confidence? *"Confidence is gained by exceeding one's own expectations."*
~~~~~~
TIME TO ASSESS:

Can you think of a time when you listened to someone's direction or someone took your direction and the course of action taken was not a good idea? Write it down.

_____

_____

_____

_____

_____

What made you (and/or the others involved) believe it would work?

_____

_____

_____

_____

_____

_____

Were you pressured into doing something you did not want to do? Perhaps, you knew it wouldn't work, but didn't say anything? Explain why.

_____

_____

_____

_____

Looking back, if you had another chance, what would you do differently?

_____

_____

_____

_____

_____

_____

_____

An effective leader applies the same principles to life, whether at work or at home.

TWO

How does your team respond to your leadership effectiveness?

Do you see your peers or spouse having an easier time at leading than you do? Do you constantly have to make sure someone has not "dropped the ball?" Sometimes people will follow out of fear. However, if they respect the person in charge the job done will be superior to the job done out of fear. Workers or family members give extra effort when they feel good about what they are doing, and in many cases, it will take less time to do the job.

How do you talk to the members on your team? Do you talk to them with respect? Do you only point out the mistakes that they make, or use a tone that belittles them? Many times, it is not what is said as much as how it is said. Let's put it this way, if you were a fly on the wall, what would you hear the people in your life say about you? Go ahead:

Write a mock letter from the hearts of your workers or family to you. Imagine what they would say.

~~~~~~

TIME TO ASSESS:

Date:_____

Dear, _____

(Look at the examples.)

Would they say?

"We love working for you, you always come up with such good ideas. Thanks for the pat on the back the other day! I was not sure if I was on the right track."

Or would they say:

"You are so hard to work with. You are moody, and I feel like I have to walk on eggshells when I am around you. I wish you would talk to me with respect. I am doing my best!"

Signed _____

If you really want to know how you are doing as a leader, ask those you are in contact with what you could do different to make their job less stressful. The following is an example of an ineffective leader.

I was working with a team one time where the leader wanted others to be responsible for their actions. However, every time he turned around, they "dropped the ball." He had to constantly micromanage everything. He was tired of that because he could not get his own work done. Poor staff retention was one of the reasons he was having such a hard time. When his workers became skilled, they left for other jobs. He never had trouble hiring more employees but finding people to stay for a long time was challenging.

Here is what happened. When this leader was young, his father was terribly hard on him. His father would tell him he was a quitter, accident prone, and that he would never amount to anything. Because this leader had, from an early age, saw himself through his father's eyes, no matter how successful the leader became, or how fast the workers worked, it was never good enough.

When he came to the job site, the entire energy of the job would change. He would inspect everything with a fine toothcomb and bark out commands and insults.

Instead of his workers feeling proud and empowered, the presence of their boss gave them anxiety, and they felt hopeless. They came to realize that no matter how hard or how much they tried; it would never be good enough.

Everyone tolerates pain differently. If you experienced this kind of leadership, especially at a young age, your self-esteem may have been impacted. You can live with emotional abuse for a long time but not be happy. In this case, you are not leading your life, life is leading you.

Are you a victim, a leader, or both? Are you a victim of your past and a leader without the respect of your employees or your family?

- An effective leader leads by example.

- An effective leader has the respect of his or her team members. Team members give their all, not out of fear, but out of respect because they know they are a part of something greater than their individual selves.

- An effective leader shows respect for each member on the team and values the natural gift or ability that each team member can offer.

- An effective leader realizes that each team member is a part that makes the whole.

- An effective leader is only as good as his or her team. The team will only be as good as his or her ability to empower each individual to be a good leader.

- An effective leader knows how to delegate, but still oversees.

- An effective leader knows how to set goals and keep the journey alive with enthusiasm and encouragement.

- An effective leader understands boundaries, his or her own as well as the personal boundaries of the team members.

☐

- An effective leader knows how to address wrong actions without disrespecting the person within.

- An effective leader takes responsibility for his or her mistakes.

- An effective leader has good discipline.

~~~~~~

TIME TO ASSESS:

Can you give an example when you could have been more effective as a leader?

_____

_____

_____

_____

Can you give an example of when you were an effective leader?

_____

_____

_____

_____

An effective leader applies the same principles to life, whether at home or at work.

Life is holographic!

If you want to help your staff or team members become effective leaders so they take on more responsibility, gift them a copy of this book. The more effective they become at meeting their own needs, the more effective they will become at meeting your needs at work.

THREE

Why will someone follow a leader even if they are not sure their idea will work?

Some people have it all when it comes to selling themselves and being an effective leader. Take for instance, Barack Obama. Even if you didn't vote for him, you have to give him credit for his style and personality. He didn't have an extensive background in the financial realm, but people trusted and believed in his ability to get us out of a recession. He had never fought in a war, but people thought he could create peace.

The reason was he was the whole package! He knew how to focus on what was important to the nation. He showed confidence and had great discipline. We heard that he spent time with his family and made time to exercise. He ate right and still had time to run our country. I don't know how he managed to maintain such balance in his life, but people liked what they heard about his personal life and liked what they saw.

Another reason our country wanted to follow him was because he made himself constantly seen and heard which reinforced our trust in him. That is called, "Top of the Mind Awareness." He appeared to be honest and caring even though a few sketchy associations came out of the woodwork. One of the things we constantly heard Barack Obama say was "Not everyone is going to be happy." That is honest!

He was very respectful of others; he had good boundaries, and we know that by watching how he conducted himself. He was enthusiastic, encouraging and he knew how to delegate and lead by example.

Barack Obama gave the American people what they wanted, so he could also give America what he thought was needed! Through television he formed a relationship with the country.

I liked to listen, and watch Barack Obama speak; as a speaker, he was brilliant. He knew when to raise and lower the volume of his voice. He always spoke in sound bites, a rhythm that is easy to hear and remember. Barack Obama had fantastic eye contact and body language when he spoke. He added stories to the point he was trying to make which made those who were listening have a better understanding and feel sympathy.

Many were unsure that his ideas would work, but his excellent leadership helped the majority of people to believe in him. He was what we needed because most of us had lost hope. Barack Obama gave us hope and encouraged us to believe.

So, why do we follow a leader even if we are not sure that his or her idea will work? Because an effective leader gives us hope and they make us feel enthusiastic about what they are proposing. An effective leader has a plan; they communicate clearly; they listen; and we are empowered to be the best that we can be. An effective leader suggests that we are part of something great and shows respect; he or she is confident and disciplined and he or she leads by example. An effective leader must be focused and have continuity whenever they are leading. Continuity gains trust and respect.

If you have a family, think about how you can use the information in this chapter to transform your family dynamics.

~~~~~~

TIME TO ASSESS:

What are some of the skills you have as a leader?

_____

_____

_____

_____

What skills do you want to gain?

_____

_____

_____

_____

An effective leader applies the same principles to life, whether at work or at home.

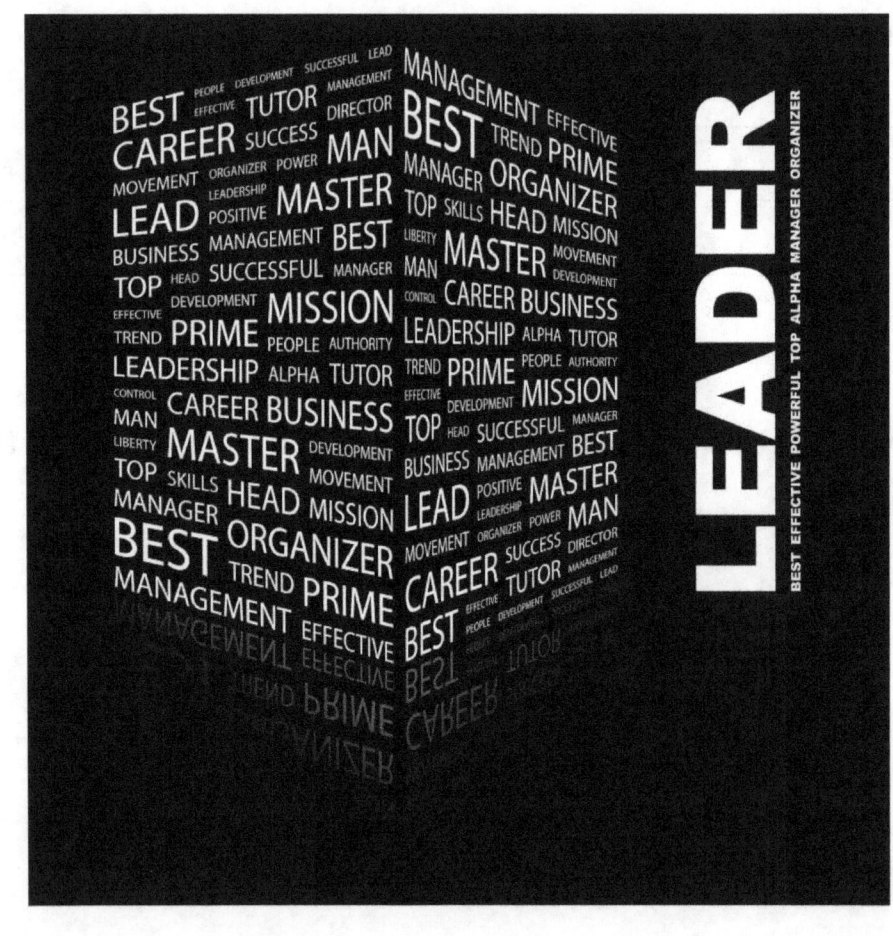

FOUR

Should the leadership role shift to other people during a project? Why?

There should always be one person who has the last word in a project or with a request. The order in command needs to be established from the start for each project. For instance, you may have to listen to your manager, but above the manager is the CEO of the project. Once the ground rules are established the company or organization that is most productive will have divisions of leaders.

In your family, your husband might be in charge of some things while you are in charge of others. It doesn't mean the other has no say in the matter; the input of both is valuable. It simply means, that in some situations you get the last word and in other situations, he gets the last word.

Delegating is a hard thing to do sometimes. It is hard when you are so invested in the outcome of a project or event. Letting others take responsibility for portions of the project can be nerve racking. Most people in charge want to continually manage every aspect of the task at hand. If you do this, you will not empower or show respect to the members of your organization or your spouse. Your team will feel like you do not trust them. An effective leader has to balance the vision or the goal of the project with confidence, encouragement, and enthusiasm while still allowing others to lead. This is why the understanding of personal boundaries is such an important skill for an effective leader.

From time to time when the members of your team meet to discuss the progress, each division is making, as the team leader you will be responsible to keep the goal in sight. In addition, the team leader must make sure everyone is "up to speed." Sometimes you will have to redirect a portion of the project that may be slipping in productivity or outcome. This needs to be said in a way that is firm and to the point without disrespecting the person who is in charge of this part of the project. That is why learning to speak about the actions of a situation, instead of the person's character is so important. It is sometimes hard to separate the two. However, an effective leader can and will develop this skill.

Here is an example: We were doing a team-building day with the faculty of a high school. Some of the personnel didn't understand why everyone had to participate. We not only had the teachers and administrators, but we also had the school nurse, janitor, coach, and the cafeteria cooks. We were working with the entire team of the school, even though they did not recognize that they were all part of the same team.

During the day, we did many different team-building initiatives. In order to be successful, we needed everyone's participation. What they learned was the important lesson of how each person affects the next. It's the ripple effect. We are each affected by each other's actions and conduct. If the janitor does not do his job or is having a bad day, it will affect the teachers, which will affect the students, which will affect the parents. Everyone is affected by the actions of others. The other lesson learned was the importance of being a leader within your own domain. The principal was the leader of the school, but it was a teacher who organized the day. Who was in charge? Who was the leader?

As long as it is communicated, different people should take the role of the leader depending on their expertise. The top leader should empower and facilitate within the team to make that happen. One of the leader's jobs is to keep the vision in view. The leader still must have the last word because he or she is the guiding force.

Why should the leadership role shift to other people during a project or job? The answer is that each person should be a leader within his or her own area. Individual rights, corporate or team divisions, and natural interests and abilities define that area. In a big company, each division will have a leader. The leader should shift the role to whomever can best accomplish the task at hand. If you are a family, you can choose one of your family members to be in charge and lead a specific job or project. On any project or job, employing the individual talents and ambitions of the entire team, will produce grander results than you could have ever imagined.

The thing to remember is that an effective leader is only as effective as his or her team; the team will only be as effective as his or her leadership ability to empower each individual to do the best job that they can do.

Here is an example: I was getting ready to go talk to an organization in New Jersey. I asked my husband, who has traveled all over the world, to make my airline reservations. He did as I asked and I "*took for granted*" that it was done correctly. We had a stopover in Denver where my best friend and assistant and I got off the plane. We went to check the departures to see the time for our next flight. She was looking at Philadelphia while I was looking at Pittsburgh.

Catharine, being from the East Coast said, "Why are you looking at Pittsburgh?" To make a long story short, we had a 6 1/2 hour drive the next morning across Pennsylvania.

The lesson is, always make the time that is needed to go over your checklist and communicate clearly what your needs are. If you are in the position to delegate or you are in charge of the big picture, remember that part of your job is making sure the task is accomplished without directing every step of the way.

~~~~~~

TIME TO ASSESS:

Can you think of a time when you took something for granted and it didn't turn out the way you had planned?

_____

_____

_____

_____

Whose fault was it? Why?

_____

_____

_____

What could you have done differently?

_____

_____

_____

_____

Since the title of this chapter is about changing leadership roles, can you think of a time when you should have delegated part of a project to someone else and failed to do so? *Write it down.*

_____

_____

_____

_____

_____

What was the lesson?

_____

_____

_____

_____

Do you have family meetings? If not, do you think they would be beneficial and why?

_____

_____

_____

_____

Do you have office meetings? Why do you think office meeting could be important? Or, why are office meetings important?

_____

_____

_____

_____

What are some good ideas that an effective leader could do to conduct an effective meeting?

_____

_____

_____

_____

_____

An effective leader applies the same principles to life, whether at work or at home.

FIVE

Why is it sometimes difficult to assume a leadership role?

If you are not confident or you do not carry through on your word, leadership will be a hard task. It all comes down to trust. If you are not trusted, you cannot lead.

Answer these five questions, be honest and you will see what kind of leader you are in this moment of time.

Write the answers down.

~~~~~~

TIME TO ASSESS:
How do you increase your level of trust in someone?

_____

_____

_____

_____

On a scale of 1 10, rate how much trust you have in your team? Can you explain your rating?

_____

_____

_____

_____

_____

_____

_____

_____

What did you do today that deserves the trust of others?

_____

_____

_____

_____

How does the amount of fear you have affect your trust in others?

_____

_____

_____

_____

Compare your answers to your personal style or character. Looking at the questionnaire and the list in the INTRODUCTION section of this book that states the qualities of a good leader. Where do you stand and what qualities do you want to improve?

_____

_____

_____

_____

So, there you have it! The answers above should give insight as to why it is sometimes difficult to assume a leadership role and whether you are ready to be an effective leader. If not, you will need to take some steps so you can lead yourself and be proactive. Then you will be ready to, lead your department or team or an entire project providing oversight each step of the way and offering others the encouragement to be effective leaders.

Being consistent is a good way to gain trust, so is following through on your word. In Chapter Ten you will discover some proven methods for gaining confidence and discipline.

An effective leader applies the same principles to life, whether at work or at home.

SIX

Why do some people take leadership roles?

There are two reasons people have a leadership role. Either the person is a Type (A) personality who naturally possesses most of the qualities we have spoken about and assumed the leadership role, or someone gave the leadership role to that person. When the second example is the reason for someone being in a leadership role, the leader invariably will show anger or upset. Having a job dropped in your lap is not by choice. A leader who has not chosen to lead will not be an effective leader.

All team members need to feel they have a choice and are valued for what they have to offer. If they do not have a choice the project, family, or organization will not succeed. This kind of situation can be very frustrating! If there is not a designated leader, two or more people will find conflict. What can you do if this is your team or organizations challenge? Your team will need to choose, a leader and lay some ground rules that everyone can agree upon. Everyone needs to feel they are in choice and that they are an important part of the plan. Always begin with the end result in mind.

Remember the teams with the most productivity, are those where individual expertise, and ambitions are committed to the same task and where each member feels valued and has a choice. If you are the leader of your team, and that is not a choice, make sure the team members feel valued and encouraged. If not, they will not be committed to the plan.

Here is an example. I was working with a group one time and one of the goals of the program was to learn how to work together as a team. They needed to learn how to "turn towards each other instead of against each other." They kept trying to do different projects, and there was a lot of conflict. What had happened was many of the leaders from the previous year had retired. The new employees and the employees that had been there for a long time were colliding with their ideas. The new workers didn't feel appreciated for what they had to contribute. According to them, the senior workers knew it all, and wouldn't listen to their ideas. According to the senior workers, they had been taught to do things a certain way, and it worked. They felt like, "Why fix it, if it ain't broke?"

I am sure you can imagine how our day went. A blending of the two was not easy. Fortunately, by the end of the day they managed to see the gift in blending their different styles, ideas, and finding appreciation with each other.

~~~~~~

TIME TO ASSESS:

What team are you a member of? (Don't forget your family.)

_____

_____

_____

_____

How can you assist the team members in appreciating each other?

_____

_____

_____

_____

What do you appreciate about your team members?

_____

_____

_____

What do you not appreciate about some of your team members?

_____

_____

_____

What is your commitment to the team? What is your vision?

_____

_____

_____

Looking at your commitment and now knowing that each member of the team needs to feel valued and in choice, in order for your commitment or vision to happen, what can you do differently?

_____

_____

_____

Can you accept others for who they are instead of who they are not? Can you give an example?

_____

_____

_____

_____

Do you feel you are a leader of something that had no choice?

_____

_____

_____

How can you find choice in being the leader? What are the gifts that go with that responsibility?

_____

_____

_____

_____

An effective leader applies the same principles to life, whether at work or at home.

SEVEN

How does it feel to follow different leaders?

Think of some of the different leaders you have had in your life.
For instance, think about your parents, teachers, coaches,
doctors, siblings, or employers. How about the different world
leaders in your lifetime?

~~~~~~

TIME TO ASSESS:
List the names of leaders you admire.

_____

_____

_____

_____

_____

What are some of the things you liked about each of their styles?
Write it down.

_____

_____

_____

_____

What are some of the things about their style you did not appreciate?

_____

_____

_____

_____

How did it feel to follow leaders you appreciate?   **Why?**

_____

_____

_____

_____

Can you think of an example when it was not a good idea to trust one of your leaders? What did they do to that made you take action?

_____

_____

_____

_____

_____

In what ways would you like to be more like those who have led you in the past?

_____

_____

_____

_____

How can you add those qualities to who you are?

_____

_____

_____

_____

How do you think it will change the dynamics of your team, including you?

_____

_____

_____

_____

An effective leader applies the same principles to life, whether at work or at home.

EIGHT:

Who sets the goals for a project, family or team?

An effective leader is confident, respectful, courteous, clear, firm, empowering, and knows how to delegate. An effective leader is always learning, has a positive mental attitude, encourages, understands boundaries, takes responsibility, is disciplined, is a good communicator, and knows how to set goals.

Setting goals is the roadmap to success. On a personal level, goals are nothing more than dreams that you want to have come true. You wouldn't get into your car and just drive aimlessly. Life is the same. If you don't have a direction you are just sightseeing, not going towards a destination. Your goal may be not to have any goals, and just go with the flow, and see how it goes. However, realize "to go with the flow and see how it goes" is a goal.

Having a mission statement gets you thinking about your direction and goals. You can create a personal mission statement, which I refer to it as your title page. As a family, you can create a mission statement together. Your business should definitely have a mission statement. Your mission statement, or personal title page, tells the world what you are committed to, or what your family is all about; your actions and conduct show that you mean what you say. By creating your personal title page or mission statement, you will see what actions you need to take and start setting your goals accordingly.

(To see my Personal Mission Statement, see page 125)

Goals should be set in each part of your life. Some categories of goals may be career, relationship, financial, health, and retirement. We make goals for our appearance, health, and family. It would be productive to set goals in each of these categories. When working on a common goal or project, each member of the team needs to set goals to achieve their part of the project.

In addition, goals can be changed if your needs change energetically.

Here is an important part of goals that people don't always understand. When you set a goal, have a time when it starts, a way to measure it and when the goal is to be completed. *"Time, Result, and Finish."* (TRF) This is so important! If you give it your all and if you don't finish in the time frame you have set, simply reset the time frame. Write down a new date of completion and when the job is completed, write that down as well. If you have done everything in your power to get the job done and you have communicated clearly and honestly to your team, most of the time something can be worked out. Also remember, a good leader knows how to delegate.

When getting ready to set your goals, write out on a sheet of paper what the result will be when you achieve your goal. How will it change your present circumstances? Your goals must be made with passionate intent. If you can't see it in your mind and really feel it perhaps, it is not a true goal. It may be something you feel you have to do or should do. Don't should on yourself! If this happens, dismiss the supposed goal, or get passionate about what the result will be.

For instance, you may not be passionate about giving up smoking, but you may be passionate about your life, your children, and not dying early from cancer.

"By the way, this is how you get into the brain set of having a choice. Choose the outcome of your choice.

~~~~~~

TIME TO ASSESS:

What are some of your goals?

_____

_____

_____

_____

What will be the result when you achieve your goal?

_____

_____

_____

_____

How will it change your present circumstances?

_____

_____

_____

_____

What will be the TRF on one of your goals?

_____

_____

_____

_____

What is your personal mission statement? *(Who you are, what you are committed to, and why.)*

_____

_____

_____

_____

_____

_____

_____

_____

_____

_____

_____

_____

_____

_____

_____

An effective leader applies the same principles to life, whether at work or at home.

NINE

What are the traits of an effective team member and are the team members as important as the leader?

The traits of an effective team member are just as important as those of an effective leader. Not everyone wants the responsibility of overseeing an entire project. Just being in charge of your own little piece of the puzzle might be enough. If that is you, you are extremely important to the progress of project.

An effective team member still needs to learn the skills of being an effective leader. Each member needs to lead his or her own life and area of expertise. A team member is just as important as a leader because without effective members a leader would not get things accomplished.

Just as the skill of communication is important to a team leader, the team member has the same responsibility to the team leader and to the rest of her team. Being part of a team has its own set of challenges. The understanding of boundaries is extremely important and being able to communicate in a way that you are heard and respected are necessary skills to be an effective team player.

Here are some questions you can ask yourself when things *"are not"* going smoothly.

~~~~~~

TIME TO ASSESS:

Have I communicated my needs to the other team members or the team leader? *(Your needs may be a vacation day, or a class you may want to take.)*

_____

_____

Did I make my request to the proper authority?

_____

_____

_____

_____

_____

If not, what has prevented me from asking?

_____

_____

_____

_____

What is the worst thing that could happen if I were to ask for what I wanted pertaining to work?

_____

_____

_____

_____

Do I need anything from my team members now? How about the person in charge of this project? If so, what?

_____

_____

_____

_____

How will I feel if I ask for what I want, and I am rejected?

_____

_____

_____

_____

Many times, people will not ask or say what they need because they are afraid of rejection. What does the word "NO" mean to you? Does it mean you are a failure or worthless? Are you afraid your request will make someone angry? Learn to make the answer "NO" not reflect on your self-worth. If you don't ask, it won't happen and being a good team member is an important role. If you are unsatisfied with the way things are going, and you don't speak up the other people involved will feel your upset and will react unfavorably. Always find the good in whatever situation and be the best you can be!

Here is a really good quote about the way others sometimes speak to us in ways we do not appreciate.

If you are willing to look at another person's behavior toward you as a reflection of the state of their relationship with themselves rather than a statement about your value as a person, then you will, over a period of time cease to react at all.
- Yogi Bhajan-

Here is something else to keep in mind. As a wife or a parent you may not realize it, but your mood sets the tone for your family. If you are not taking time for yourself, you will not be the family leader that you want to be. Every morning and before you get home from work, take five minutes to focus on what you look forward to when you see your family. They will all have needs as soon as you see them. Just like your co-workers they are looking for direction. You will have to shift gears and if you have had a hard day think about what you are grateful for. Then if it is too much to deal with, tell your family that you need to go for a walk or relax before you can help them. Part of being a good leader is to set an example. Taking time for yourself is critical for your success. Your energy and mood will affect the success of your requests. See Chapter Thirteen for more information on Self-Care.

An effective leader applies the same principles to life, whether at work or home.

TEN

How can you improve your ability to take direction and improve your listening skills?

As you are now aware, whether you are a leader or a team member the same skills need to be learned. If you really want to improve your ability to take direction, tune up your listening skills. We have two ears and one mouth for this reason: we need to listen more.

How often do people tell you something and you would swear you have never heard it before? A good leader shows respect and encourages others to do his or her best. If you do not listen to the members of your team, they will feel unvalued and will stop trying. You will lose trust and credibility. One answer to this problem is to have regular meetings so you can focus on the challenge your team is having. Another is using a method to make sure everyone has his or her say. I have used a "talking stick" in both my family and my business meetings. Find a method that works for you.

Think about the answers to the questions below. Are you a good listener?

Write in the answers.

~~~~~~

TIME TO ASSESS:

What is your method for keeping track and do you acknowledge those who share different ideas?

_____

_____

_____

_____

Do you hear all the different ideas? How do you know?

_____

_____

_____

_____

Why are some suggestions ignored without being acknowledged?

_____

_____

_____

_____

What interferes with your ability to listen?

_____

_____

_____

_____

How can this interference be overcome?

_____

_____

_____

_____

Do you prevent yourself from listening?   How?

_____

_____

_____

_____

_____

Following can be hard for some people. They struggle with taking direction. If you are one of those, can you figure out why?

Do you have a hard time taking direction? If so, why?

_____

_____

_____

_____

_____

When do you choose to take direction?

_____

_____

_____

_____

When do you choose not to take direction? Why?

_____

_____

_____

_____

If you want to be part of a team or community and you want to be valued, learn the skills of being an effective member and leader.

An effective leader applies the same principles to life, whether at work or at home.

ELEVEN

What does it take to be an effective leader?

I hope you now understand the basics of leadership. Each person has to be a leader of his or her own destiny, and it starts with a goal. On a group project, it is best to have one main leader that holds the goal in sight. The main leader has the last word. She has to connect on a personal level, find out her teams' needs, acknowledge the good and redirect her as needed. The team needs to realize there are choices. Team members need to join forces on a common goal with his or her individual talents and ambitions for something worthwhile to happen.

The skills that are needed to be an effective leader, and member of a team are:

- Leading by example.

- Empowering others.

- Expanding your mind and knowledge.

- Having a strong positive mental attitude.

- Sharing enthusiasm and encouragement.

- Creating good, clear boundaries.

- Taking responsibility for your own mistakes.

- Being a good listener.

- Communicating clearly.

- Confidence.

- Delegating.

- Setting goals.

- Showing respect.

- Understanding.

- Passion.

A great leader has good discipline, and people skills.

Most of these skills can be a conditioned response. A conditioned response is something that you learn. It becomes part of your character. Confidence and discipline are two skills you need to gain. You have read in this book that, *"Confidence is gained by exceeding one's own expectations."* Gaining discipline and confidence can be a challenge. They go hand-n-hand, because if you gain confidence, you have exceeded your own expectations. In order, to exceed your own expectations you need to stay with a project or a goal until it is complete, and that takes discipline. If you are challenged when it comes to having discipline, make consequences for yourself if you do not follow through.

In addition, tell your consequences to someone else so you are accountable.

Here is an example: I always tell my son when I need to commit to something that I need to do, but don't want to do. I can't lie to my son. Usually I tell him when I am about to go on a diet. My consequence is something I don't ever want to do, but it is not harmful. This is what I usually tell him. "If I don't stick to a certain eating plan and exercise at least thirty minutes everyday, for an extended amount of time, I will eat the sickest wet cat food of his choice." I call all my diets the cat food diet because of the agreement I make with him. If I can get my son to commit to something, he is trying to accomplish it makes it even more interesting and fun!

This is what works for me. Of course, you don't have to eat something sick. You could say if you don't *"do whatever"* you will donate your time to a charity or clean the cages at the zoo or wash the other person's car.

Get creative! You also need to talk on the phone once a
week to hold each other accountable and to report your progress.
Make sure you have a date to begin and a date to be complete.
(TRF)

If you want to build your confidence, set small goals and work up
to larger ones. I needed to prove to myself when I reached the age
of thirty-five that if I put my mind to it, I could do anything. I
needed that extra shot of confidence. I was working many
challenge courses at the time. Climbing high in the trees and
walking on cables and jumping off what we called, "The Trapeze
Leap" (which was an element, forty feet in the air) was not a
challenge for me. I needed to really push my limit.

I thought about it for a while and then decided I would
accomplish five things. #1, I would finally do a back dive, off the
diving board into the swimming pool. I had tried for years and
always held myself back. I did five back dives.
#2, I would publish a poem and I did. #3, I would run a 6-k. I keep
the picture next to my bed. #4, I would work full time.   I found
that having two young children, being married, keeping a home,
and garden, including mowing my own lawns, and working at a
preschool four hours a day, was more than full time. #5, I would
jump out of an airplane.
That's right, I jumped out of a perfectly good airplane at
12,000 feet.

If you want to build your confidence, make a list of things you will
accomplish by a certain date. Little bits at a time your discipline
and confidence will become stronger. I don't suggest you "start"
with jumping out of an airplane. However, I do suggest that you
start doing small things and work yourself up to more difficult
challenges.

~~~~~~

TIME TO ASSESS:

What are some things you can do to build your confidence?

_____

_____

_____

_____

_____

What areas of your life do you want to gain more discipline?

_____

_____

_____

_____

What will it do to benefit you?

_____

_____

_____

_____

How would your life be affected if you had more discipline and confidence?

_____

_____

_____

_____

An effective leader applies the same principles to life, whether at work or at home.

TWELVE

Common challenges both women and men face

See if any of these apply to

- You are working full time and still doing most of the domestic chores.

- You are working full time and still doing most of the childcare.

- You don't have any personal time.

- You and your true love don't have time to make love.

- Sharing the role of leadership with your spouse is challenging.

- The needs of your spouse, family, and even the animals seem to come before yours.

- You are ready for change, but you don't want to rock the boat.

- After working all day, doing homework with the children, making dinner, and doing chores your partner gets angry because you don't want to make love.

- Your children won't do the chores you have asked them to do.

- Your children won't bring home their homework assignments.

- You and your spouse are not on the same page when it comes to childcare.

- You know how to be a leader at work, but at home you don't know how to be loving and still be a leader.

- You are responsible for too many things.

- Your mate or children are not listening to you.

- You have to be too may places at one time.

- Your "better half," expects everything to be completed when he or she gets home from work.

- You say yes to things you want to say no to because you want to be nice and not cause an upset.

- You are a people pleaser

- You are not passionate about your job or family.

- Your fellow team members don't follow through.

- There is too much bickering happening at work or at home.

- Your team members or family are not working well together. There is not enough teamwork.

- Communication seems to be broken down.

If you said yes to any of the scenarios above, here is the answer.

An effective leader applies the same principles to life, whether at work or at home.

If you want to be an effective leader, an effective coach, own a business, or have a great family life, co-create with your team members. Learn how to make your team members feel valued. If you are a parent that is married, co-create with your spouse and give your kids choices. The choice can be, either you bring your homework home each day and do it, or you stay in on the weekends and get it done. Decide your direction, what you want from life, what you want for your family and let your goals dictate your actions.

On a project at work talk to your team regularly so they feel valued. You don't have to share every detail because some of your business is not for them to know. However, share the parts that are important to the success of their department.

It may be easier to be more giving and loving when you are at home than at work. But your boundaries and the way you conduct yourself must remain the same. Otherwise, your team or family will second guest you, and you will have conflict. Stand firm in your direction. Life is like a "holograph." You are the same person in every situation. If you think you are one way at work and another way at home, you are mistaken. Every person we have conflict with is a mirror for us to see ourselves.

Lead your life, or life will lead you. Make the information in this book a conditioned response. A conditioned response is a new way to react to stimuli that comes your way.

In addition, take care of yourself. If you take care of yourself, you will be giving permission for others to take care of themselves. When you take care of your needs with exercise, your spiritual life, eating right, sharing time with friends or taking a class you want to take, you are in balance. Being in balance is important to being valued as a great leader. If you do not value yourself enough to do things that you enjoy you are not leading your life. n the next chapter we will discuss the importance of Self-Care.

An effective leader applies the same principles to life, whether at work or at home.

THIRTEEN

How Self-Care Works with Leadership

I am a coach and a woman. Most of my clients are looking for ways to keep up with a full life without the drain of exhaustion, health issues, and the challenges of keeping the family unit functioning. The pressures of a full life take a toll on human physiology and can block your need to be on top of your game and mentally fit. We are all looking for ways to make life work.

As an adult, we wear many hats. I had a nightgown once that said, mother, wife, executive, psychologist, manager, nurse, gardener, veterinarian, and the list went on, and it was true. As a woman we do it all.

Caring for ourselves, and those around us is an important skill in being an effective leader.

As women we care from the depth of our souls; from the core of our hearts. We sometimes care so much that we over-care to the point that we don't leave anytime for ourselves.

Care is a form of passion. However, if we get over attached to the outcome and forget about the journey, we end up feeling over-whelmed and anxious.

Over-caring for others causes stress, overload, and overwhelm. It starts out with the best intentions, but unmanaged it becomes a mental and emotional drain.

This goes for men as well. We all have male and female energy Some men are very caring, loving, and nurturing when it comes to relationships and family. Self-care needs to be an important part of their lives as well.

When was the last time you did something just for you? The best leaders are those who have balance in their lives. They make their needs just as important as their team members and families. In a sense, they have it all.

Women and men, do it all, and can have it all if they learn techniques to eliminate stress, enhance their decision-making and improve their performance.

~~~~~~

TIME TO ASSESS:

Is what you care about adding quality to your life?
Explain.

_____

_____

_____

_____

_____

What are you doing that is not worthy of your time?

_____

_____

_____

_____

_____

What worries can you let go?

_____

_____

_____

_____

In the past, what did you do to relieve stress?

_____

_____

_____

_____

What are some things you can do to relieve stress?

_____

_____

_____

What would you lose and gain if you took time for yourself?

_____

_____

_____

_____

When was the last time you had quality time with your loved ones?

_____

_____

_____

_____

What dreams do you have for the future and what is holding you back?

_____

_____

_____

Is there something you have wanted to do for yourself?   What is it?

_____

_____

_____

_____

What are some things that you enjoy?

_____

_____

_____

_____

_____

_____

What have you been feeling guilty about not doing?

_____

_____

_____

_____

_____

What scares you about the future?

_____

_____

_____

_____

_____

An effective leader applies the same principles to life, whether at work or at home.

Once you begin your journey in Self-Care you will find freedom and joy in your choices. With that you will rediscover more energy and passion for life. Reading _"Be a Leader in All that You Do,"_ is a good first step in enriching your life and stepping into your role as a leader. However, if you really want to lead your life effectively, and have a powerful team, give yourself and your team members the gift of this book.

FOURTEEN

Managing Stress

How do you manage stress? You will need to come up with a plan so when you feel irritated, you can turn it around before you get upset.

I am a licensed Heartmath Institute trainer, coach and mentor. I show people techniques they can use so their minds can stay clear and focused. When you get upset the brain stops thinking clearly and Intuition shuts down. The Heartmath techniques can be applied and shared with those in your family or where you work. It is scientifically proven to relieve stress. I teach some of the techniques whenever I do a leadership or equine assisted training. That way besides discovery, people can walk away from the day with a new tool in their imaginary toolbox of coping skills.

There are many ways to relieve stress so you can be more productive and an effective leader. What can you do when you feel stress?

Write them down.

_____

_____

_____

_____

_____

_____

FIFTEEN

Knowing How to Facilitate is Good Leadership.

In my book, "The Art of Facilitation with 28 Equine Assisted Activities I give the facilitator who is the leader of a training, over a dozen categories of questions that can be asked when leading people in a task.

The questions are similar to the questions I ask you in this book? Like we mentioned earlier, people need to feel they are in choice. One of the ways to do this is to learn the art of facilitation.

The categories include:

Communicating effectively
Expressing appropriate feelings
Deferring judgement on others
Appreciating self and others
Leading others
Following others
Asking for what you want
Closing Questions

Making group decisions
Liking yourself
Listening
Cooperating
Respecting commonalities
Respecting differences
Trusting the group

All Categories that an Effective Leader needs to Consider and be Able to Speak to when Leading a Team or Project.

CONCLUSION

_____

WHAT happened?

SO WHAT, did you discover about yourself?

NOW WHAT, changes are you going to make?

Assessing your leadership style: What's working and What's not?

~~~~~~-

TIME TO ASSESS:

What do you think? Where do you see some areas of your life that needs some fine-tuning?

_____

_____

_____

_____

So what did you discover about your past leadership style?

_____

_____

_____

_____

Now what are you going to do different?

_____

_____

_____

How are you going to apply the information you have just read in "Be a Leader in All that You Do?"

_____

_____

_____

How can you apply the information in this book to any of the situations in your life?

_____

_____

_____

What are some things you are going to do for yourself?

_____

_____

_____

What will you change today? Starting today I will?

_____

_____

_____

_____

If you want to be an effective leader, you have to dare to dream. You need to set your sights and make a plan. Learn to think about what can be done in every situation. Always come up with at least ten possible solutions; even if you think the answer is not a possibility, write it down. Be a creative problem solver and if you truly want to change be accountable with someone who shares your best interest.

Whenever you come to what looks like a roadblock on your journey, pretend like you are in a bubble, looking for the way out. When you find the soft spot; the point of least resistance, pop it and move forward. Ask yourself how can this dilemma be changed? What can you do to change the circumstances? What are your options? Just keep asking yourself what else you can do? Find a way to tackle the challenge that is holding you back from reaching your goal.

"Lead your Life of Life will Lead You!"

Qualities of an Effective Leader

- An effective leader leads by example.

- An effective leader has the respect of her team members. Team members give their all, not out of fear, but out of respect because they know they are a part of something greater than their individual selves.

- An effective leader shows respect for each member on the team and values the natural gift or ability that each team member can offer.

- An effective leader realizes that each team member is a part that makes the whole.

- An effective leader is only as good as his or her team. The team will only be as good as his or her ability to empower each individual to be a good leader.

- An effective leader knows how to delegate, but still oversees.

- An effective leader knows how to set goals and keep the journey alive with enthusiasm and encouragement.

- An effective leader understands boundaries, his or her own as well as the personal boundaries of the team members.

- An effective leader knows how to address wrong actions without disrespecting the person within.

- An effective leader takes responsibility for his or her mistakes.

- An effective leader has good discipline. An

  effective leader can be anyone.

- An effective leader applies the same rules to his or her life, at work and at home.

An effective leader applies the same principles to life, whether at work or at home.

Leadership Assessment Strategies

Do you have what it takes to be a leader or a coach? Do you have what it takes to be part of a team? Do you have what it takes to let go of your ego and hear constructive criticism? Do you have what it takes to lead your life into the future? There is a leadership role for you in all aspects of your life, whether it is in your *Work, Family, Friendships, Community*, or your *Self-Care.*

The rest of this book is for you to keep track of when you were an effective leader. When confrontation, conflict or struggle occurs, write down what happened, how you handled the situation, and what you learned from the experience. Then strategize a plan for the next time a similar situation occurs to be more effective.
Keep track of your progress and date the entries. Like anything worth doing, it will take time to change the way you have been doing things in life. In the past it was suggested that it takes 28 days to change. However, more recent studies show it takes 18 days or as many as 245 days.

Life is a dance; Enjoy the process!

Change the way you look at things and things you look at change.
~Jack Canfield~

Watch your thoughts they become words.
Watch your words they become actions.
Watch your actions they become habits.
Watch your habits they become character.
Watch your character it becomes your destiny.
~Dali Lama~

If you think you handle life differently in your work and family what you need to realize is life is holographic. You may be more lenient or show more caring actions in part of your life however, the way you process life's situations will remain the same. Your same challenges will show up in all realms of your life.

"No matter where you go, there you are."

DATE - WHAT HAPPENED - HOW DID YOU HANDLE THE SITUATION - WHAT DID YOU LEARN - HOW COULD YOU HAVE HANDLED IT DIFFERENTLY?

_____

_____

_____

_____

_____

_____

_____

_____

_____

_____

_____

_____

_____

DATE - WHAT HAPPENED - HOW DID YOU HANDLE THE SITUATION - WHAT DID YOU LEARN - HOW COULD YOU HAVE HANDLED IT DIFFERENTLY?

_____

_____

_____

_____

_____

_____

_____

_____

_____

_____

_____

_____

_____

DATE - WHAT HAPPENED - HOW DID YOU HANDLE THE SITUATION - WHAT DID YOU LEARN - HOW COULD YOU HAVE HANDLED IT DIFFERENTLY?

_____

_____

_____

_____

_____

_____

_____

_____

_____

_____

_____

_____

DATE - WHAT HAPPENED - HOW DID YOU HANDLE THE SITUATION - WHAT DID YOU LEARN - HOW COULD YOU HAVE HANDLED IT DIFFERENTLY?

_____

_____

_____

_____

_____

_____

_____

_____

_____

_____

_____

_____

_____

_____

DATE - WHAT HAPPENED - HOW DID YOU HANDLE THE SITUATION - WHAT DID YOU LEARN - HOW COULD YOU HAVE HANDLED IT DIFFERENTLY?

_____

_____

_____

_____

_____

_____

_____

_____

_____

_____

_____

_____

_____

DATE - WHAT HAPPENED - HOW DID YOU HANDLE THE SITUATION - WHAT DID YOU LEARN - HOW COULD YOU HAVE HANDLED IT DIFFERENTLY?

_____

_____

_____

_____

_____

_____

_____

_____

_____

_____

_____

_____

_____

DATE - WHAT HAPPENED - HOW DID YOU HANDLE THE SITUATION - WHAT DID YOU LEARN - HOW COULD YOU HAVE HANDLED IT DIFFERENTLY?

_____

_____

_____

_____

_____

_____

_____

_____

_____

_____

_____

_____

_____

DATE - WHAT HAPPENED - HOW DID YOU HANDLE THE SITUATION - WHAT DID YOU LEARN - HOW COULD YOU HAVE HANDLED IT DIFFERENTLY?

_____

_____

_____

_____

_____

_____

_____

_____

_____

_____

_____

_____

_____

DATE - WHAT HAPPENED - HOW DID YOU HANDLE THE SITUATION - WHAT DID YOU LEARN - HOW COULD YOU HAVE HANDLED IT DIFFERENTLY?

_____

_____

_____

_____

_____

_____

_____

_____

_____

_____

_____

_____

DATE - WHAT HAPPENED - HOW DID YOU HANDLE THE SITUATION - WHAT DID YOU LEARN - HOW COULD YOU HAVE HANDLED IT DIFFERENTLY?

_____

_____

_____

_____

_____

_____

_____

_____

_____

_____

_____

_____

_____

DATE - WHAT HAPPENED - HOW DID YOU HANDLE THE SITUATION - WHAT DID YOU LEARN - HOW COULD YOU HAVE HANDLED IT DIFFERENTLY?

_____

_____

_____

_____

_____

_____

_____

_____

_____

_____

_____

_____

_____

DATE - WHAT HAPPENED - HOW DID YOU HANDLE THE SITUATION - WHAT DID YOU LEARN - HOW COULD YOU HAVE HANDLED IT DIFFERENTLY?

_____

_____

_____

_____

_____

_____

_____

_____

_____

_____

_____

_____

_____

DATE - WHAT HAPPENED - HOW DID YOU HANDLE THE SITUATION - WHAT DID YOU LEARN - HOW COULD YOU HAVE HANDLED IT DIFFERENTLY?

_____

_____

_____

_____

_____

_____

_____

_____

_____

_____

_____

_____

DATE - WHAT HAPPENED - HOW DID YOU HANDLE THE SITUATION - WHAT DID YOU LEARN - HOW COULD YOU HAVE HANDLED IT DIFFERENTLY?

_____

_____

_____

_____

_____

_____

_____

_____

_____

_____

_____

_____

_____

_____

DATE - WHAT HAPPENED - HOW DID YOU HANDLE THE SITUATION - WHAT DID YOU LEARN - HOW COULD YOU HAVE HANDLED IT DIFFERENTLY?

_____

_____

_____

_____

_____

_____

_____

_____

_____

_____

_____

_____

_____

DATE - WHAT HAPPENED - HOW DID YOU HANDLE THE SITUATION - WHAT DID YOU LEARN - HOW COULD YOU HAVE HANDLED IT DIFFERENTLY?

_____

_____

_____

_____

_____

_____

_____

_____

_____

_____

_____

_____

_____

DATE - WHAT HAPPENED - HOW DID YOU HANDLE THE SITUATION - WHAT DID YOU LEARN - HOW COULD YOU HAVE HANDLED IT DIFFERENTLY?

_____

_____

_____

_____

_____

_____

_____

_____

_____

_____

_____

_____

_____

DATE - WHAT HAPPENED - HOW DID YOU HANDLE THE SITUATION - WHAT DID YOU LEARN - HOW COULD YOU HAVE HANDLED IT DIFFERENTLY?

_____

_____

_____

_____

_____

_____

_____

_____

_____

_____

_____

_____

_____

DATE - WHAT HAPPENED - HOW DID YOU HANDLE THE SITUATION - WHAT DID YOU LEARN - HOW COULD YOU HAVE HANDLED IT DIFFERENTLY?

_____

_____

_____

_____

_____

_____

_____

_____

_____

_____

_____

_____

_____

DATE - WHAT HAPPENED - HOW DID YOU HANDLE THE SITUATION - WHAT DID YOU LEARN - HOW COULD YOU HAVE HANDLED IT DIFFERENTLY?

_____

_____

_____

_____

_____

_____

_____

_____

_____

_____

_____

_____

_____

DATE - WHAT HAPPENED - HOW DID YOU HANDLE THE SITUATION - WHAT DID YOU LEARN - HOW COULD YOU HAVE HANDLED IT DIFFERENTLY?

_____

_____

_____

_____

_____

_____

_____

_____

_____

_____

_____

_____

DATE - WHAT HAPPENED - HOW DID YOU HANDLE THE SITUATION - WHAT DID YOU LEARN - HOW COULD YOU HAVE HANDLED IT DIFFERENTLY?

_____

_____

_____

_____

_____

_____

_____

_____

_____

_____

_____

_____

_____

DATE - WHAT HAPPENED - HOW DID YOU HANDLE THE SITUATION - WHAT DID YOU LEARN - HOW COULD YOU HAVE HANDLED IT DIFFERENTLY?

_____

_____

_____

_____

_____

_____

_____

_____

_____

_____

_____

_____

DATE - WHAT HAPPENED - HOW DID YOU HANDLE THE SITUATION - WHAT DID YOU LEARN - HOW COULD YOU HAVE HANDLED IT DIFFERENTLY?

_____

_____

_____

_____

_____

_____

_____

_____

_____

_____

_____

_____

DATE - WHAT HAPPENED - HOW DID YOU HANDLE THE SITUATION - WHAT DID YOU LEARN - HOW COULD YOU HAVE HANDLED IT DIFFERENTLY?

_____

_____

_____

_____

_____

_____

_____

_____

_____

_____

_____

_____

_____

DATE - WHAT HAPPENED - HOW DID YOU HANDLE THE SITUATION - WHAT DID YOU LEARN - HOW COULD YOU HAVE HANDLED IT DIFFERENTLY?

_____

_____

_____

_____

_____

_____

_____

_____

_____

_____

_____

_____

DATE - WHAT HAPPENED - HOW DID YOU HANDLE THE SITUATION - WHAT DID YOU LEARN - HOW COULD YOU HAVE HANDLED IT DIFFERENTLY?

_____

_____

_____

_____

_____

_____

_____

_____

_____

_____

_____

_____

_____

DATE - WHAT HAPPENED - HOW DID YOU HANDLE THE SITUATION - WHAT DID YOU LEARN - HOW COULD YOU HAVE HANDLED IT DIFFERENTLY?

_____

_____

_____

_____

_____

_____

_____

_____

_____

_____

_____

_____

DATE - WHAT HAPPENED - HOW DID YOU HANDLE THE SITUATION - WHAT DID YOU LEARN - HOW COULD YOU HAVE HANDLED IT DIFFERENTLY?

_____

_____

_____

_____

_____

_____

_____

_____

_____

_____

_____

_____

_____

DATE - WHAT HAPPENED - HOW DID YOU HANDLE THE SITUATION - WHAT DID YOU LEARN - HOW COULD YOU HAVE HANDLED IT DIFFERENTLY?

_____

_____

_____

_____

_____

_____

_____

_____

_____

_____

_____

_____

_____

DATE - WHAT HAPPENED - HOW DID YOU HANDLE THE SITUATION - WHAT DID YOU LEARN - HOW COULD YOU HAVE HANDLED IT DIFFERENTLY?

_____

_____

_____

_____

_____

_____

_____

_____

_____

_____

_____

_____

_____

DATE - WHAT HAPPENED - HOW DID YOU HANDLE THE SITUATION - WHAT DID YOU LEARN - HOW COULD YOU HAVE HANDLED IT DIFFERENTLY?

_____

_____

_____

_____

_____

_____

_____

_____

_____

_____

_____

_____

_____

_____

DATE - WHAT HAPPENED - HOW DID YOU HANDLE THE SITUATION - WHAT DID YOU LEARN - HOW COULD YOU HAVE HANDLED IT DIFFERENTLY?

_____

_____

_____

_____

_____

_____

_____

_____

_____

_____

_____

_____

_____

DATE - WHAT HAPPENED - HOW DID YOU HANDLE THE SITUATION - WHAT DID YOU LEARN - HOW COULD YOU HAVE HANDLED IT DIFFERENTLY?

_____

_____

_____

_____

_____

_____

_____

_____

_____

_____

_____

_____

DATE - WHAT HAPPENED - HOW DID YOU HANDLE THE SITUATION - WHAT DID YOU LEARN - HOW COULD YOU HAVE HANDLED IT DIFFERENTLY?

_____

_____

_____

_____

_____

_____

_____

_____

_____

_____

_____

_____

DATE - WHAT HAPPENED - HOW DID YOU HANDLE THE SITUATION - WHAT DID YOU LEARN - HOW COULD YOU HAVE HANDLED IT DIFFERENTLY?

_____

_____

_____

_____

_____

_____

_____

_____

_____

_____

_____

_____

DATE - WHAT HAPPENED - HOW DID YOU HANDLE THE SITUATION - WHAT DID YOU LEARN - HOW COULD YOU HAVE HANDLED IT DIFFERENTLY?

_____

_____

_____

_____

_____

_____

_____

_____

_____

_____

_____

_____

_____

_____

DATE - WHAT HAPPENED - HOW DID YOU HANDLE THE SITUATION - WHAT DID YOU LEARN - HOW COULD YOU HAVE HANDLED IT DIFFERENTLY?

_____

_____

_____

_____

_____

_____

_____

_____

_____

_____

_____

_____

_____

DATE - WHAT HAPPENED - HOW DID YOU HANDLE THE SITUATION - WHAT DID YOU LEARN - HOW COULD YOU HAVE HANDLED IT DIFFERENTLY?

_____

_____

_____

_____

_____

_____

_____

_____

_____

_____

_____

_____

DATE - WHAT HAPPENED - HOW DID YOU HANDLE THE SITUATION - WHAT DID YOU LEARN - HOW COULD YOU HAVE HANDLED IT DIFFERENTLY?

_____

_____

_____

_____

_____

_____

_____

_____

_____

_____

_____

_____

_____

DATE - WHAT HAPPENED - HOW DID YOU HANDLE THE SITUATION - WHAT DID YOU LEARN - HOW COULD YOU HAVE HANDLED IT DIFFERENTLY?

_____

_____

_____

_____

_____

_____

_____

_____

_____

_____

_____

_____

_____

DATE - WHAT HAPPENED - HOW DID YOU HANDLE THE SITUATION - WHAT DID YOU LEARN - HOW COULD YOU HAVE HANDLED IT DIFFERENTLY?

_____

_____

_____

_____

_____

_____

_____

_____

_____

_____

_____

_____

_____

DATE - WHAT HAPPENED - HOW DID YOU HANDLE THE SITUATION - WHAT DID YOU LEARN - HOW COULD YOU HAVE HANDLED IT DIFFERENTLY?

_____

_____

_____

_____

_____

_____

_____

_____

_____

_____

_____

_____

_____

DATE - WHAT HAPPENED - HOW DID YOU HANDLE THE SITUATION - WHAT DID YOU LEARN - HOW COULD YOU HAVE HANDLED IT DIFFERENTLY?

_____

_____

_____

_____

_____

_____

_____

_____

_____

_____

_____

_____

_____

DATE - WHAT HAPPENED - HOW DID YOU HANDLE THE SITUATION - WHAT DID YOU LEARN - HOW COULD YOU HAVE HANDLED IT DIFFERENTLY?

_

_____

_____

_____

_____

_____

_____

_____

_____

_____

_____

_____

DATE - WHAT HAPPENED - HOW DID YOU HANDLE THE SITUATION - WHAT DID YOU LEARN - HOW COULD YOU HAVE HANDLED IT DIFFERENTLY?

_____

_____

_____

_____

_____

_____

_____

_____

_____

_____

_____

_____

_____

DATE - WHAT HAPPENED - HOW DID YOU HANDLE THE SITUATION - WHAT DID YOU LEARN - HOW COULD YOU HAVE HANDLED IT DIFFERENTLY?

_____

_____

_____

_____

_____

_____

_____

_____

_____

_____

_____

_____

DATE - WHAT HAPPENED - HOW DID YOU HANDLE THE SITUATION - WHAT DID YOU LEARN - HOW COULD YOU HAVE HANDLED IT DIFFERENTLY?

_____

_____

_____

_____

_____

_____

_____

_____

_____

_____

_____

_____

DATE - WHAT HAPPENED - HOW DID YOU HANDLE THE SITUATION - WHAT DID YOU LEARN - HOW COULD YOU HAVE HANDLED IT DIFFERENTLY?

_____

_____

_____

_____

_____

_____

_____

_____

_____

_____

_____

_____

_____

DATE - WHAT HAPPENED - HOW DID YOU HANDLE THE SITUATION - WHAT DID YOU LEARN - HOW COULD YOU HAVE HANDLED IT DIFFERENTLY?

_____

_____

_____

_____

_____

_____

_____

_____

_____

_____

_____

_____

_____

BOOKS INCLUDE:

Be a Leader in All that You Do,
A Self-Exam of your Leadership Effectiveness.

The Art of Facilitation, with 28 Equine Assisted Activities.
(This book is your safety net when doing equine assisted programs)

Words Hit Hard as a Fist, with 18 Tips on How to STOP being Bullied.

The Secret Daydream, A Guide to your Child's Future. *(The children's version of the best selling 2006, self-help book "**The Secret**," which has sold over 19 million copies worldwide. "**The Secret Daydream**," was written in fable and beautifully illustrated by the author.)*

Charisse Rudolph's Personal Mission Statement

My Mission Statement is to stay in balance while earning enough money to answer my needs. I will do this by giving the most efficient service I am capable of giving. What I give in service, I will gain in financial rewards, staying true to whom I am and the abilities I can share. I will pay it forward when I can, and I will love and be loved.

www.ingramcontent.com/pod-product-compliance
Lightning Source LLC
Chambersburg PA
CBHW080641180526
45168CB00008B/3259